SARIKA FRIEND-ZONED

BY MANISH

(SPECIALLY FOR BRAVE READERS)

BY

DR. AMIT JAYANT DESHMUKH

SHOOLIN
PRESS
MUMBAI, MAHARASHTRA

ISBN: 978-81-993067-4-5

Edition: 2025

Publisher: **Shoolin Press**
Mumbai, Maharashtra
E-mail: shoolinpressinfo@gmail.com

DISCLAIMER

All the names, characters, businesses, places, events and incidents which are mentioned in this book are either the author's imagination or used in a fictitious manner. Any resemblance to actual persons, living or dead or actual events is purely coincidental.

Author Info

DR. Amit jayant deshmukh

Qualifications - B.com., M.a. Philosophy, Religion And Culture, Ph.d. In Philosophy, Certified Astrologer, Palm Reader, Numerologist, Yoga, Philosopher, Meditation Teacher, Insurance Agent, Mutual Fund Distributor And Spiritualist

Contact :- 9702837022 / 8265056254

Email: 16108adad@gmail.com

Table Of Contents

CHAPTER ONE

HER STORY

Sarika and Ayush were working for the same company since the last seven months. Ayush's mother came to know from the other sources that Sarika's mother is her childhood friend who lived in the same locality. This story is mainly about the interesting events which happen in the Sarika's life. Initially, Sarika and Ayush did not have the idea that their mothers are childhood friends. Her story may entertain and educate the readers.

Ayush comes to know after seven months that his mother and Sarika's mother are childhood friends who lived in the same locality. It was such a coincidence. Destiny plays a very major role in the life of the human beings which is based on their activities performed in the previous births. The scientific proof of rebirth is given by Ian Stevenson, Jim Tucker and Doctor Satwant Pasricha.

The scriptural proof of rebirth in given in the Bhagavadgita, chapter number two and verse number twenty-seven. The law of karma controls the destiny of the persons in this material world. The law of karma is very complex and cannot easily be understood by the people of this material world as mentioned in the seventeen's verse of the fourth chapter of Bhagavadgita.

Destiny means those incidents which happen in the lives of people which are completely beyond their control. The references of verses from scriptures like Bhagavadgita are mentioned in this book to give Shabda Pramaana which is the scriptural evidence as per the subject of Philosophy which is the mother of all the subjects. Philosophy is considered the mother of all subjects because it gives us the permanent solution of moksha to solve the main problems of life which are common for all the humans.

Moksha means permanently getting out of the repeated cycle of rebirth and death. Birth, old age, disease and death are the main problems of life because these problems are common for all the persons in this material world as per the Bhagavadgita, chapter 13, verse number 9. The verses of the scriptures do not change. The translations, purports and commentaries of the verses mentioned in different scriptures may change.

Ideally, only those commentaries of scriptures should be considered authentic if they are according to the Guru-shishya Parampara (a chain of disciplic succession of spiritual master and their disciples). Chanting and trying to attentively hear mantras which are mentioned in the scriptures can help the people in this age of kaliyug to attain moksha (liberation from material bondage).

The Hare Krushna mantra is given in kali santarana Upanishad of Krushna Yajurveda. Atleast one round or maalaa of Hare Krushna mantra meditation daily may prepare the person for obtaining moksha. If a person at the time of death is able to chant and hear the Hare Krushna mantra, he or she has a chance to get permanently out of the repeated cycle of rebirth and death. One who remembers God, Krushna at the time of death can get moksha as mentioned in the fifth verse, eighth chapter of Bhagavadgita.

www.vedabase.com is one of the bonafide website which contains the knowledge given in various scriptures. According to the law of destiny, two persons may meet coincidentally to sort out the pending transactions of life. A child may take birth in the family of those parents who are indebted to him or her in some previous birth. Too many coincidences were happening in the lives of both Sarika and Ayush.

Sarika started approaching Ayush very frequently. She is an extrovert by nature. She liked talking to him and being around him. It may be a connection with him because of samskaaraas of some previous birth. The samskaaraas are the impressions on the subconscious mind of an individual which suddenly creates an attraction towards the unknown person. She felt that she has met him before.

It was a feeling of déjà vu (experienced earlier) for her. She started showing mixed feelings for him. Mixed feelings are about showing sudden interest in him and after some time showing a kind of indifference towards Ayush. She had the habit of playing mind-games. Sometimes, she used to become angry without any reason. No one was able to pacify her because its funny to understand that she did not know the actual reason for her anger.

Generally, people want to love someone or something and have the desire that their liking should be reciprocated by the other person. She is an attention seeker. The employees who worked with Sarika and Ayush also came to know that their mothers are childhood friends who stayed in the same locality. The other employees started to tease Sarika and Ayush. They started encouraging both Sarika and Ayush to get involved in a romantic relationship.

Sarika and Ayush were linked (paired) with each other. Sarika had the habit of wearing those dresses whose colour was related to the planet which ruled on a particular day according to the concept of numerology. Sarika was wearing pure-white coloured dress on Mondays, red coloured dress on Tuesdays, green coloured dress on Wednesdays, yellow coloured dress on Thursdays of every week, off-white and cream-coloured dresses on Fridays and black or blue coloured dresses on the Saturdays.

- ✓ Monday represents pure-white colour because it is ruled by the moon
- ✓ Tuesday represents the red (blood) and a combination of colours as it is related to the planets named as the Mars and ketu
- ✓ Wednesday represents the green colour which is ruled by mercury

- ✓ Thursday represents the yellow colour as it is ruled by the Jupiter planet
- ✓ Friday represents the off-white and cream colours as it is ruled by venus
- ✓ Saturday represents the black or blue colours because it is related to the planets like Saturn and rahu

Sarika wanted Ayush to notice her choices related to the colour of her dresses and in this way enjoy life. It was her desire to impress Ayush. She wanted to give proof to Ayush that she is a very sincere follower of the subject of numerology. Sarika and Ayush both had the knowledge of the subject of numerology.

- ➢ Monday represents number two
- ➢ Tuesday represents number nine
- ➢ Wednesday represents number five
- ➢ Thursday represents number three
- ➢ Friday represents number six
- ➢ Saturday represents number eight
- ➢ Sunday represents number one which is ruled by the sun planet.

Ayush was not aware of what was Sarika wearing on Sundays because he never got the opportunity to see her dress on the Sundays. He was curious to know about the colour which she was wearing on the Sundays. There may be a famous proverb which is related to the word of 'Curiosity'. The proverb is called as the 'Curiosity kills the cat'. Sarika had many male friends in the company.

She had the habit of associating with the male employees in that company. She would generally prefer being with male employees of that company. One day she walked up to Ayush and told him in a very straightforward way that if she decides to befriend some person, she will make sure to have that individual in her life. She had informed Ayush that she considered him as her friend.

She appeared to be too demanding at times. She started taking Ayush for granted. She had the false ego that Ayush is by-default her friend. Ayush did not like this kind of a forceful friendship of Sarika. Ayush was spiritually inclined. He knew that every living being is a finite spiritual soul embodied in the material bondage of the repeated cycle of rebirth and death. The reference for the fact that I am not the material body but I am is finite spiritual soul in given in the Bhagavadgita, chapter number two and verse number 13.

"dehino 'smin yathā dehe
kaumāraṁ yauvanaṁ jarā
tathā dehāntara-prāptir
dhīras tatra na muhyati

Synonyms

dehinaḥ — of the embodied; asmin — in this; yathā — as; dehe — in the body; kaumāram — boyhood; yauvanam — youth; jarā — old age; tathā — similarly; deha-antara — of transference of the body; prāptiḥ — achievement; dhīraḥ — the sober; tatra — thereupon; na — never; muhyati — is deluded.

Translation

As the embodied soul continuously passes, in this body, from boyhood to youth to old age, the soul similarly passes into another body at death. A sober person is not bewildered by such a change.” [1]

Ayush was having the philosophical knowledge that the finite spiritual soul is permanently a part of the Supreme God, Krushna as mentioned in the Bhagavadgita, chapter number fifteen and verse number seven. He also was aware of the fact that the finite spiritual soul is actually an eternal subordinate of the supreme lord, Krushna as mentioned in the scripture named as the Shri Chaitanya Charitamrita, Madhya leela section, chapter number twenty, verse numbers 108 and 109.

Sarika did not have this kind of a deep philosophical knowledge based on the authority of the scriptures. She would worship any Demigod (devataa) without any scriptural proof which is called as sentimentalism or fanaticism. Religion without philosophy is called as the sentimentalism or fanaticism. Philosophy without religion is called as mental or intellectual speculation.

Philosophy and religion both are equally important to attain liberation from the material existence as per the scriptures. Manish was one of the Sarika’s closest friends in that company. Manish was already married and had two children. Manish

1 Prabhupāda, A.C. Bhaktivedānta Swāmi. ‘Bhagavad-gītā as it is.’ Bhaktivedānta Vedabase, https://vedabase.io/en/library/bg/2/13/. Accessed 21 Sep. 2024

was unfortunately forced to marry his wife because of the demand of his parents. Manish did not like the girl whom he got married. Manish felt jealous of people who are unmarried.

Manish felt that unmarried persons are happier than him. Ayush and Sarika were both unmarried. Manish wanted Ayush and Sarika to marry each other. Manish felt that he is doing a pious (punya) work by trying to create a link-up between Ayush and Sarika. Sometimes, Manish would try to make Ayush jealous by saying that Manish would have married Sarika if Manish was unmarried.

Manish would call both Ayush and Sarika at a staff room in the company near Manish's desk at the same time. Manish would ask Ayush whether Sarika looked beautiful or not. Sarika was inquisitive to know how many men are attracted to her. Sarika was checking her validity by trying to impress men of that company. Sarika wanted to see if men of that company find her irresistible or not.

The employees of that company were gossip lovers who called any kind of gossip as the **"Juicy gossip"**. Sarika was a very hardcore attention seeker especially from the male employees of that particular company. Vinay was one of the senior employees of that company. Vinay sir had the opinion about Sarika that she can never become a faithful and chaste wife. Vinay sir felt that Sarika does not have the good qualities of chastity, submissiveness and loyalty which is very important to live a good married life.

Sarika had advised Ayush that he should never get married to a girl who is too younger in age as compared to him. Many of the employees of that company felt that Sarika and Ayush should get married to each other because both of them had so many similarities. Sarika and Ayush had a common interest in occult sciences like numerology and predicting the future events in the life of any individual.

Ayush felt that Sarika was not a real spiritualist because of the fact that she was worshipping the one of the Demigod (Devataa). A demigod or a demigoddess is generally worshipped by a person who wants too many material benedictions as the knowledge of Bhagavadgita, chapter number seven and verse number twenty.

"kāmais tais tair hṛta-jñānāḥ
prapadyante 'nya-devatāḥ
taṁ taṁ niyamam āsthāya
prakṛtyā niyatāḥ svayā

Synonyms

kāmaiḥ — by desires; taiḥ taiḥ — various; hṛta — deprived of; jñānāḥ — knowledge; prapadyante — surrender; anya — to other; devatāḥ — demigods; tam tam — corresponding; niyamam — regulations; āsthāya — following; prakṛtyā — by nature; niyatāḥ — controlled; svayā — by their own.

Translation

Those whose intelligence has been stolen by material desires surrender unto demigods and follow the particular rules and regulations of worship according to their own natures." [2]

Ayush was aware that the demigods and the demigoddesses cannot liberate the people from the repeated cycle of rebirth and death. Ayush had the opinion that Sarika was more emotional and less practical because she never followed the authority of scriptures which is one of the strongest proofs in the subject of Philosophy. Ayush felt that Sarika was taking the biggest risk by not worshipping the supreme God (Krushna or Vishnu and their avataars or incarnations) as mentioned in the Bhagavadgita, chapter number 18 and verse number 66.

Meanwhile, Sarika was confused about her own relationship status as she had the difficulty in deciding whether to get into a romantic relationship or not.

Sarika's female friends were mostly divorcees. In the modern age of kaliyug, it had become very difficult to maintain a marriage after getting married. Sarika would sometimes advise Ayush to remain unmarried. Sarika would sometimes feel that since Ayush's nature was very good, he could become an ideal husband. Sarika had sent some whatsapp messages to Ayush that he had a good chance to settle.

---

2 Prabhupāda, A.C. Bhaktivedānta Swāmi. 'Bhagavad-gītā as it is.' Bhaktivedānta Vedabase, https://vedabase.io/en/library/bg/7/20/. Accessed 24 Sep. 2024

However, Ayush was thinking that getting married would be risky for his spiritual life as the material necessities usually increase after marriage. Sarika sometimes had the habit of getting angry without any logical reason. It was difficult to pacify Sarika when she became angry. Sarika had mood swings and so was very unpredictable regarding her behaviour with people. Sarika would smile when she met people.

Sarika revealed the fact that she has experienced a lot of unhappiness even though she had the habit of smiling in difficult situations. Sarika desired relationships as strong as that button which is depicted in the image that is given below.

I Want a relationship as strong as that button

The reference for the above-mentioned image is as follows - **content://media/external/downloads/472271**

Sarika once informed Ayush that she wanted to marry a man whose income is as much as her income (equal money). Ayush thought that after Sarika's marriage, if she starts earning more money than her would-be husband or if her would-be husband became jobless, Sarika may become dissatisfied with her would-be husband. Ayush thought that it may be very risky to marry a person like Sarika.

Ayush had the opinion that Sarika may behave more like a boss and less like a wife with her husband in case she gets married. Interestingly, Sarika was planning to work in some other company. Sarika would frequently inform Ayush that she may shift to some other company. Ayush felt that may be Sarika is trying to check whether Ayush may propose her to get involved in a romantic relationship or not because of the feeling of separation if she shifts to some other company.

Ayush thought about the concept of Syadvada in Jain philosophy. Syat means 'may be' in the Sanskrit language. Ayush thought about different probabilities or 'may be's' regarding Sarika's frequent statements informing Ayush about her possibility to change the job. Ayush's prediction may be correct or wrong. Manish told Ayush that if Sarika joins some other company, Manish will definitely miss her.

Ayush felt that this may be a strategy of both Manish and Sarika to create a romantic attraction in the mind of Ayush towards Sarika by trying to make Ayush feel jealous or possessive. Sarika may want to check if Ayush becomes crazy about her after hearing about her change of job. All these possibilities are the guess-works of Ayush which may be correct or wrong.

Generally, people may infer that wherever there is smoke, there has to be fire. This inference may be correct or wrong because sometimes it appears like smoke but it may actually be fog especially during the winter season.

❁❁❁

CHAPTER TWO

PERMANENT RELATIONSHIP STATUS

Sarika would often encourage Ayush that he may get a permanent job in the future if he keeps trying for it. Ayush felt that there is no unconditional love in this material world. If a person is rich, people are ready to marry him or her. Till the time a person is able to fulfill the expectations, he or she will be liked and respected in this material world. Permanent job appears very tempting, lucrative and attractive because of the possibility of the constant source of income.

The suffering in a so-called permanent job is also a fact in this material world. Honestly, no job in this material world is permanent because every person has to leave his or her material body at the time of death. Actually, Sarika's permanent relationship status is only with the supreme God as mentioned in the scriptures like Shri Chaitanya Charitamrita, Madhya leela section, chapter number twenty and verse numbers 108 and 109.

"jīvera 'svarūpa' haya — kṛṣṇera 'nitya-dāsa'
kṛṣṇera 'taṭasthā-śakti' 'bhedābheda-prakāśa'

sūryāṁśa-kiraṇa, yaiche agni-jvālā-caya
svābhāvika kṛṣṇera tina-prakāra 'śakti' haya

Synonyms

jīvera — of the living entity; svarūpa — the constitutional position; haya — is; kṛṣṇera — of Lord Kṛṣṇa; nitya-dāsa — eternal servant; kṛṣṇera — of Lord Kṛṣṇa; taṭasthā — marginal; śakti — potency; bheda-abheda — one and different; prakāśa — manifestation; sūrya-aṁśa — part and parcel of the sun; kiraṇa — a ray of sunshine; yaiche — as; agni-jvālā-caya — molecular particle of fire; svābhāvika — naturally; kṛṣṇera — of Lord Kṛṣṇa; tina-prakāra — three varieties; śakti — energies; haya — there are.

Translation

"It is the living entity's constitutional position to be an eternal servant of Kṛṣṇa because he is the marginal energy of Kṛṣṇa and a manifestation simultaneously one with and different from the Lord, like a molecular particle of sunshine or fire. Kṛṣṇa has three varieties of energy." [3]

Sarika had a dream of getting married to the Pakistani cricketer named as Shahid Afridi. Sarika had written (SSA) inside her bedroom in her childhood. The full form of (SSA) is Sarika Shahid Afridi. Sarika was also attracted to the other Pakistani

3 Prabhupāda, A.C. Bhaktivedānta Swāmi. 'Shri Chaitanya Charitamrita.' Bhaktivedānta Vedabase, https://vedabase.io/en/library/cc/madhya/20/108-109/. Accessed 26 Sep. 2024

cricketers like Imran Khan and Wasim Akram. Sarika was especially crazy about the bowling style of both these Pakistani fast bowlers named as the Imran Khan and Wasim Akram.

There is a very important purport given by A.C. Bhaktivedanta Swami Prabhupada (founder-acharya of International society for Krishna consciousness) regarding this topic which is mentioned in one of the verse of the scripture named as the Bhagavata Purana.

"kasyā manas te bhuvi bhogi-bhogayoḥ
striyā na sajjed bhujayor mahā-bhuja
yo 'nātha-vargādhim alaṁ ghṛṇoddhata-
smitāvalokena caraty apohitum

Synonyms

kasyāḥ — whose; manaḥ — mind; te — your; bhuvi — in this world; bhogi-bhogayoḥ — like the body of a serpent; striyāḥ — of a woman; na — not; sajjet — becomes attracted; bhujayoḥ — by the arms; mahā-bhuja — O mighty-armed; yaḥ — one who; anātha-vargā — of poor women like me; adhim — distresses of the mind; alam — able; ghṛṇā-uddhata — by aggressive mercy; smita-avalokena — by attractive smiling; carati — travels; apohitum — to dissipate.

Translation

O mighty-armed, who in this world will not be attracted by your arms, which are just like the bodies of serpents? Actually you relieve the distress of husbandless women like us by your attractive smile and your aggressive mercy. We think that you are traveling on the surface of the earth just to benefit us only.

Purport

When a husbandless woman is attacked by an aggressive man, she takes his action to be mercy. A woman is generally very much attracted by a man's long arms. A serpent's body is round, and it becomes narrower and thinner at the end. The beautiful arms of a man appear to a woman just like serpents, and she very much desires to be embraced by such arms. The word anātha-vargā is very significant in this verse.

Nātha means "husband," and a means "without." A young woman who has no husband is called anātha, meaning "one who is not protected." As soon as a woman attains the age of puberty, she immediately becomes very much agitated by sexual desire. It is therefore the duty of the father to get his daughter married before she attains puberty. Otherwise she will be very much mortified by not having a husband.

Anyone who satisfies her desire for sex at that age becomes a great object of satisfaction. It is a psychological fact that when a woman at the age of puberty meets a man and the man satisfies her sexually, she will love that man for the rest of her life, regardless who he is. Thus so-called love within this material world is nothing but sexual satisfaction." [4]

Sarika was an expert in friend-zoning men. Ayush felt that this is a type of hypocrisy in the current age to consider the

4 Prabhupāda, A.C. Bhaktivedānta Swāmi. 'Bhāgavata Purāṇa.' Bhaktivedānta Vedabase, https://vedabase.io/en/library/sb/4/25/42/. Accessed 5 Oct. 2024

members of the opposite-gender as only a friend (FRIEND ZONE). Girls in a college generally have this habit of maintaining friendship with boys. They say that, “We are just good friends and nothing more than that”. The fact is that the boy who is a friend of a girl is actually a boyfriend.

He is a boy and her friend, so he is actually her boyfriend. The reality is that these college girls have many boyfriends at the same time. Due to this kind of a hypocrisy, they want to avoid a serious commitment with many boyfriends simultaneously but have an intense desire to associate with the people of the opposite-gender. This process is called as the **benching**. Benching is about friend-zoning many people of the opposite gender at a given time.

Because of such a behaviour and so-called free-culture, it has become very difficult to minimize the material pleasures which is very important for the purpose of spiritual advancement. If a person of the opposite gender who is friend-zoned currently starts earning more money, then the friend may become best-friend (**BFF – best-friend forever**) or **boyfriend** or **fiancé** or **husband** for the reason of securing the future.

Sarika was addicted to drinking tea. Sarika came to know from Manish that Ayush never had tea till now in his life-time ever. Sarika desperately felt the need to permanently give-up the habit of tea-addiction. Sarika was trying to give-up tea after she got inspired by observing Ayush. Sarika tried to refrain from drinking tea for a period of approximately one week by trying to imitate Ayush.

After that, Sarika was not able to come for work for two days because she suffered from withdrawal symptoms for suddenly trying to give-up the tea addiction.

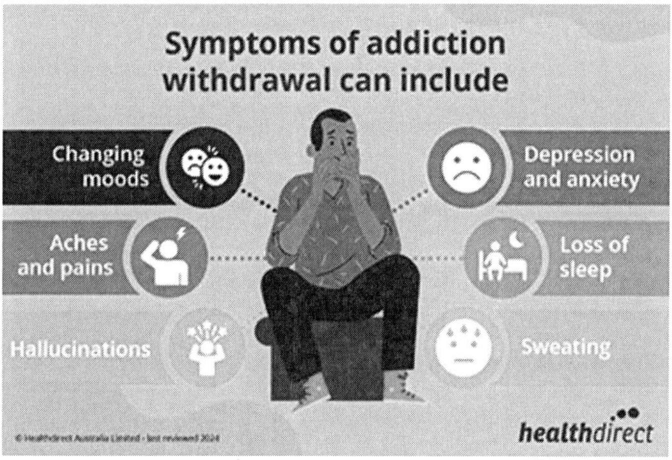

Old habits die hard. It is very difficult to give-up the bad habits and unwanted addictions because of the withdrawal symptoms. Similarly, it is also difficult to overcome the illusory energy of the supreme God which is called as the **maahaa-maayaa** as mentioned in the Bhagavadgita, chapter number seven and verse number fourteen. A person who has surrendered or is sincerely trying to surrender to the supreme God, Krushna can very easily cross beyond the influence of the material energy of the supreme God, Krushna.

"daivī hy eṣā guṇa-mayī
mama māyā duratyayā
mām eva ye prapadyante
māyām etāṁ taranti te

Synonyms

daivī ***— transcendental;*** ***hi*** ***— certainly;*** ***eṣā*** ***— this;*** ***guṇa-mayī*** ***— consisting of the three modes of material nature;*** ***mama*** ***— My;*** ***māyā*** ***— energy;*** ***duratyayā*** ***— very difficult to overcome;*** ***mām*** ***— unto Me;*** ***eva*** ***— certainly;*** ***ye*** ***— those who;*** ***prapadyante*** ***— surrender;*** ***māyām etām*** ***— this illusory energy;*** ***taranti*** ***— overcome;*** ***te*** ***— they.***

Translation

This divine energy of Mine, consisting of the three modes of material nature, is difficult to overcome. But those who have surrendered unto Me can easily cross beyond it." [5]

The best way to surrender to the supreme God, Krushna is by chanting and trying to attentively hear those holy names of God, Krushna which are mentioned in the authoritative scriptures which are like the law-books for the people. Sarika was confused about her relationship status. Manish was insisting that Sarika should get married as soon as possible. Manish was Sarika's best friend in that company.

Manish and Sarika were like the character names of Rahul and Anjali in the Bollywood movie which was named as **'Kuch kuch hota hai'.** There was a famous dialogue in that movie which was named as 'Kuch kuch hota hai'**.** The dialogue was as follows – "Kuch Kuch hota hai Anjali, tum nahi samjhogi and kuch kuch hota hai Rahul, Tum nahi samjhoge". The translation from hindi to English language is as follows -

5 Prabhupāda, A.C. Bhaktivedānta Swāmi. 'Bhagavad-gītā as it is.' Bhaktivedānta Vedabase, https://vedabase.io/en/library/bg/7/14/. Accessed 6 Oct. 2024

"Something happens Anjali, you will not understand and something happens Rahul, you will not understand."

Manish was a prankster in the staff room of that company. Manish encouraged Ayush to get into a physical relationship with Sarika. Manish felt that Sarika may be feeling 'Kuch kuch hota hai' for Ayush. 'Kuch kuch hota hai' means 'Something happens'. Manish felt that something is happening related to the physical desires of Sarika. According to Manish, a lady's physical desires are more compared to that of a man's physical desires. There are references in scriptures like Bhaagavata puraana about the physical desires of a lady.

"vibhajya navadhātmānaṁ
mānavīṁ suratotsukām
rāmāṁ niramayan reme
varṣa-pūgān muhūrtavat

Synonyms

vibhajya — having divided; nava-dhā — into nine; ātmānam — himself; mānavīm — the daughter of Manu (Devahūti); surata — for sex life; utsukām — who was eager; rāmām — to his wife; niramayan — giving pleasure; reme — he enjoyed; varṣa-pūgān — for many years; muhūrtavat — like a moment.

Translation

After coming back to his hermitage, he divided himself into nine personalities just to give pleasure to Devahūti, the daughter of Manu, who was eager for sex life. In that way he enjoyed with her for many, many years, which passed just like a moment.

Purport

Here the daughter of Svāyambhuva Manu, Devahūti, is described as suratotsuka. After traveling with her husband all over the universe, in Mount Meru and the beautiful gardens of the heavenly kingdoms, she naturally became sexually stimulated, and in order to satisfy her sexual desire, Kardama Muni expanded himself into nine forms. Instead of one, he became nine, and nine persons had sexual intercourse with Devahūti for many, many years.

It is understood that the sexual appetite of a woman is nine times greater than that of a man. That is clearly indicated here. Otherwise, Kardama Muni would have had no reason to expand himself into nine. Here is another example of yogic power. As the Supreme Personality of Godhead can expand Himself in millions of forms, a yogī can also expand up to nine forms, but not more than that.

Another example is that of Saubhari Muni; he also expanded himself into eight forms. But however powerful a yogī may be, he cannot expand himself into more than eight or nine forms. The Supreme Personality of Godhead, however, can expand Himself into millions of forms, ananta-rūpa — innumerable, countless forms — as stated in the Brahma-saṁhitā. No one can compare to the Supreme Personality of Godhead by any conceivable energetic manifestation of power." [6]

Manish felt that satisfying a lady is definitely not an easy job.

6 Prabhupāda, A.C. Bhaktivedānta Swāmi. 'Bhāgavata Purāṇa.' Bhaktivedānta Vedabase, https://vedabase.io/en/library/sb/3/23/44/. Accessed 10 Oct. 2024

Women generally have more monetary expenses compared to that of men. Shopping, beauty parlours, new dresses, ornaments, make-up, I-phones and sandals with high heels are the attractions of women in general. Men are generally attracted to playing sports and reading newspapers. Sarika was confused about her true relationship status.

Sarika had never studied the scriptures which are like the lawbooks for the human beings. This is the actual reason for Sarika's ignorance about her permanent or eternal relationship with the supreme God. All relationships in this material world are temporary because every person has to die in this material world. The permanent solution to get out of the repeated cycle of rebirth and death is by attaining liberation (moksha). Sarika was too attached to her parents. Sarika did not have the feeling of renunciation or detachment from this material world. Since Sarika did not gain philosophical knowledge by studying the scriptures, she felt that her relationship status is complicated.

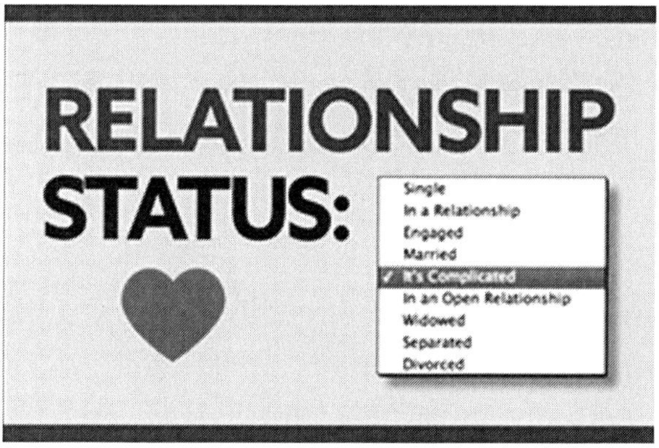

Manish claimed that he had the ability to give six kisses in a span of three seconds. Manish knew the art of flirting with girls and aunties. Manish claimed that he is an aunty-lover. Manish and Sarika, both of them were extremely talkative by nature. Manish and Sarika are best friends. Sarika would help Manish in completing his annual reports in that company. Sarika had informed Ayush that she has already helped Manish to submit his annual assignments to his departmental head.

Sarika wanted to check whether Ayush becomes jealous or not after knowing about her closeness towards Manish. Sarika wanted to check whether Ayush starts liking her or not. Sarika was playing mind-games with Ayush. Ayush felt that till the time he doesn't have a permanent job, Sarika will not be interested in getting married to him. Ayush wished that Sarika should never be interested in getting married to him.

Ayush wished that Sarika should never be interested in developing a romantic relationship with him. Ayush wanted to focus on God consciousness based on the teachings of the authentic scriptures. If a person is keen on maintaining friendship with many people of the opposite gender, he or she may consider many people as their spouse or life partner. Kaliyug is an age of degradation so anything can happen.

Very few couples are loyal and faithful to each other. This friend-zoning is a way of intimate interaction with the opposite gender by avoiding the responsibility of married life. In the ancient times, a boy and a girl would rarely communicate with each other before getting married. This kind of a culture was adopted to minimize the tendency to enjoy materialistic pleasures by creating certain strict rules between a girl and a boy.

In the modern age, the less intelligent people have neglected the scriptural rules. A boy and a girl are mostly allowed to mix freely with each other in the modern times.

"pravṛttiṁ ca nivṛttiṁ ca
janā na vidur āsurāḥ
na śaucaṁ nāpi cācāro
na satyaṁ teṣu vidyate

Synonyms

pravṛttim — acting properly; ca — also; nivṛttim — not acting improperly; ca — and; janāḥ — persons; na — never; viduḥ — know; āsurāḥ — of demoniac quality; na — never; śaucam — cleanliness; na — nor; api — also; ca — and; ācāraḥ — behavior; na — never; satyam — truth; teṣu — in them; vidyate — there is.

Translation

Those who are demoniac do not know what is to be done and what is not to be done. Neither cleanliness nor proper behavior nor truth is found in them.

Purport

In every civilized human society there is some set of scriptural rules and regulations which is followed from the beginning. Especially among the Āryans, those who adopt the Vedic civilization and who are known as the most advanced civilized peoples, those who do not follow the scriptural injunctions are supposed to be demons. Therefore it is stated here that the demons do not know the scriptural rules, nor do they have any inclination to follow them.

Most of them do not know them, and even if some of them know, they have not the tendency to follow them. They have no faith, nor are they willing to act in terms of the Vedic injunctions. The demons are not clean, either externally or internally. One should always be careful to keep his body clean by bathing, brushing teeth, shaving, changing clothes, etc. As far as internal cleanliness is concerned, one should always remember the holy names of God and chant Hare Kṛṣṇa, Hare Kṛṣṇa, Kṛṣṇa Kṛṣṇa, Hare Hare/ Hare Rāma, Hare Rāma, Rāma Rāma, Hare Hare.

The demons neither like nor follow all these rules for external and internal cleanliness. As for behavior, there are many rules and regulations guiding human behavior, such as the Manu-saṁhitā, which is the law of the human race. Even up to today, those who are Hindu follow the Manu-saṁhitā. Laws of inheritance and other legalities are derived from this book. Now, in the Manu-saṁhitā it is clearly stated that a woman should not be given freedom.

That does not mean that women are to be kept as slaves, but they are like children. Children are not given freedom, but that does not mean that they are kept as slaves. The demons have now neglected such injunctions, and they think that women should be given as much freedom as men. However, this has not improved the social condition of the world. Actually, a woman should be given protection at every stage of life.

She should be given protection by the father in her younger days, by the husband in her youth, and by the grownup sons in her old age. This is proper social behavior according to the Manu-saṁhitā. But modern education has artificially devised a puffed-up concept of womanly life, and therefore marriage is practically now an imagination in human society. The social condition of women is thus not very good now, although those who are married are in a better condition than those who are proclaiming their so-called freedom.

The demons, therefore, do not accept any instruction which is good for society, and because they do not follow the experience of great sages and the rules and regulations laid down by the sages, the social condition of the demoniac people is very miserable." [7]

The faithfulness has decreased in the married life because of unrestricted mixing between men and women. Sarika would often approach Ayush. Ayush rarely approached Sarika in the staff room. Sarika felt that Ayush is silent. Mind of a person is such that it craves for attention from that individual who is not giving much attention. Sarika is an attention-seeker by nature. Sarika felt comfortable among men of that company.

Sarika felt that female employees of that company were mostly jealous of her. Sarika belonged to a very rich family. Sarika had the habit of living life in a very high standard by spending a lot of money. Sarika had the habit of going to the pubs. A pub is generally a place where people go to buy and drink alcohol and which also serves food. Sarika felt that she

7 Prabhupāda, A.C. Bhaktivedānta Swāmi. 'Bhagavad-gītā as it is.' Bhaktivedānta Vedabase, https://vedabase.io/en/library/bg/16/7/. Accessed 15 Oct. 2024

had better facilities than that of her female employees in that company.

Sarika felt that the she looked more beautiful compared to that of the female employees in that company. Sarika had informed Ayush that she was ready to get involved in bad politics in that employee if needed. Sarika wanted to survive in a job which pays her a lot of money. Sarika felt that befriending male of employees of that company may be beneficial for her survival in that company.

Sarika wanted protection from the male employees of that company. Sarika wanted protection from bad politics in that company. Sarika was in relationship with two boys in the past. Manish was insisting Sarika to consider Ayush as her Boyfriend number 3. Vicky was Sarika's first Boyfriend. Sarika had to break her relationship with Vicky because of his over-possessive nature.

Vicky was like the character named as 'Rahul' from the Bollywood movie named as 'Darr'. This character of Rahul was played by the Bollywood actor named as 'Shah rukh Khan'. Sarika preferred that her Boyfriend should not have facial hair (beard and moustache) at all. Sarika like clean-shaved Boyfriends because she thought that they looked cute and like a chocolate boy.

She felt that Bollywood actors like Aamir Khan and Shahid Kapoor looked cute and can be called as chocolate boys according to her. Sarika was initially in relationship with two Boyfriends at the same time. Sarika was confused regarding her relationship status as she felt that she is attracted to both her boyfriends simultaneously. Sarika's second boyfriend's name was Suresh.

In the Bhagavata puran scripture, it is mentioned in one of the verses that the relationship between a man and a woman in Kaliyuga will be mostly based on superficial attraction.

"दाम्पत्येऽभिरुचिर्हेतुर्मायैव व्यावहारिके ।
स्त्रीत्वे पुंस्त्वे च हि रतिर्विप्रत्वे सूत्रमेव हि ॥ ३ ॥

dāmpatye 'bhirucir hetur
māyaiva vyāvahārike
strītve puṁstve ca hi ratir
vipratve sūtram eva hi

Synonyms

dām-patye — in the relationship of husband and wife; abhirucih — superficial attraction; hetuḥ — the reason; māyā — deceit; eva — indeed; vyāvahārike — in business; strītve — in being a woman; puṁstve — in being a man; ca — and; hi — indeed; ratiḥ — sex; vipratve — in being a brāhmaṇa; sūtram — the sacred thread; eva — only; hi — indeed.

Translation

Men and women will live together merely because of superficial attraction, and success in business will depend on deceit. Womanliness and manliness will be judged according to one's expertise in sex, and a man will be known as a brāhmaṇa just by his wearing a thread.

Purport

Just as human life as a whole has a great and serious purpose — namely spiritual liberation — fundamental human institutions such as marriage and child-rearing should also be dedicated to that great objective. Unfortunately, in the present age the satisfaction of the sex impulse has become the overriding, if not the exclusive, reason for marriage. The sexual impulse, which induces the male and female of almost every species to combine physically, and in higher species also emotionally, is ultimately not a natural urge, because it is based on the unnatural identification of the self with the body.

Life itself is a spiritual phenomenon. It is the soul that lives and gives apparent life to the biological machine called the body. Consciousness is the soul's manifest energy, and thus consciousness, awareness itself, is originally an entirely spiritual event. When life, or consciousness, is confined within a biological machine and falsely mistakes itself to be that machine, material existence occurs and sex desire arises.

God intends human life to be an opportunity for us to rectify this illusory mode of existence and return to the vast satisfaction of pure, godly existence. But because our identification with the material body is a long historical affair, it is difficult for most people to immediately break free from the demands of the materially molded mind. Therefore the Vedic scriptures prescribe sacred marriage, in which a so-called man and a so-called woman may combine in a regulated, spiritual marriage sheltered by overarching religious injunctions.

In this way the candidate for self-realization who has selected family life can derive adequate satisfaction for his senses and simultaneously please the Lord within his heart by obeying religious injunctions. The Lord then purifies him of material desire.

In Kali-yuga this deep understanding has been almost lost, and, as stated in this verse, men and women combine like animals, solely on the basis of mutual attraction to bodies made of flesh, bone, membrane, blood and so on. In other words, in our modern, godless society the weak, superficial intelligence of humanity rarely penetrates beyond the gross physical covering of the eternal soul, and thus family life has in most cases lost its highest purpose and value.

A corollary point established in this verse is that in the Age of Kali a woman is considered "a good woman" if she is sexually attractive and, indeed, sexually efficient. Similarly, a sexually attractive man is "a good man." The best example of this superficiality is the incredible attention twentieth-century people give to materialistic movie stars, music stars and other prominent figures in the entertainment industry.

In fact, pursuing sexual experiences with various types of bodies is similar to drinking old wine from new bottles. But few people in the Kali-yuga can understand this. Finally, this verse states that in the Age of Kali a man will become known as a priest, or brāhmaṇa, merely by wearing ceremonial dress. In India, brāhmaṇas wear a sacred thread, and in other parts of world members of the priestly class have other ornaments and symbols.

But in the Age of Kali the symbols alone will suffice to establish a person as a religious leader, despite his ignorance of God." [8]

Sarika was in a romantic relationship with her second boyfriend named as Suresh for approximately seven long years. Sarika claimed that she never was in a physical relationship with any of her boyfriends. The employees of that company did not completely trust her so-called platonic way of being in romantic relationship with both boyfriends at the same time. Sarika had ended both her romantic relationships because of disagreements.

Manish was advising Sarika to consider Ayush as her life-partner. Manish said that he will pay for all the expenses if Sarika and Ayush go out of lunch and dinner in any restaurant. Manish was ready to pay for Ayush's marriage related expenses if Ayush agrees to marry Sarika. Manish had a so-called permanent job in that company because of the reservation facility given to certain persons.

Manish earned a very high source of income and also a regular monthly income. Still, Manish was asking money from Sarika to pay his loans and Sarika paid many of Manish's expenses as a nice friend would help during emergency. Sarika's first boyfriend named as Vicky was behaving in an extremely romantic way with her.

Vicky had written many so-called love-letters to Sarika. True love is rarely to be experienced in this material world. The first

8 Prabhupāda, A.C. Bhaktivedānta Swāmi. 'Bhāgavata Purāṇa.' Bhaktivedānta Vedabase, https://vedabase.io/en/library/sb/12/2/3/. Accessed 2 Nov. 2024

sentence in the love-letter written by Vicky to Sarika was done using the scarlet-red coloured ink-pen. The second sentence in the love-letter written by Vicky to Sarika was done using the dark-red coloured ink-pen. The third sentence in the love-letter written by Vicky to Sarika was done using the wine-red violet coloured ink-pen.

The fourth sentence in the love-letter written by Vicky to Sarika was done using the plum violet coloured ink-pen. The next sentence in the love-letter written by Vicky to Sarika was done using the eggplant violet coloured ink-pen. The next sentence in the love-letter written by Vicky to Sarika was done using the grape violet coloured ink-pen. The next sentence in the love-letter written by Vicky to Sarika was done using the purple violet coloured ink-pen.

The next sentence in the love-letter written by Vicky to Sarika was done using the lavender violet coloured ink-pen. The next sentence in the love-letter written by Vicky to Sarika was done using the carnation pink coloured ink-pen. The next sentence in the love-letter written by Vicky to Sarika was done using the strawberry pink coloured ink-pen. The next sentence in the love-letter written by Vicky to Sarika was done using the fuchsia pink coloured ink-pen.

The next sentence in the love-letter written by Vicky to Sarika was done using the salmon pink coloured ink-pen. The next sentence in the love-letter written by Vicky to Sarika was done using the orange-coloured ink-pen. The next sentence in the love-letter written by Vicky to Sarika was done using the melon orange coloured ink-pen. The next sentence in the love-letter written by Vicky to Sarika was done using the yellow-coloured ink-pen.

The next sentence in the love-letter written by Vicky to Sarika was done using the lemon yellow-coloured ink-pen. The next sentence in the love-letter written by Vicky to Sarika was done using the lime green coloured ink-pen. The next sentence in the love-letter written by Vicky to Sarika was done using the fresh grass green coloured ink-pen. The next sentence in the love-letter written by Vicky to Sarika was done using the dark green coloured ink-pen.

The next sentence in the love-letter written by Vicky to Sarika was done using the moss green coloured ink-pen. The next sentence in the love-letter written by Vicky to Sarika was done using the green-yellow coloured ink-pen. The next sentence in the love-letter written by Vicky to Sarika was done using the sea green-blue coloured ink-pen. The next sentence in the love-letter written by Vicky to Sarika was done using the blue-green coloured ink-pen.

The next sentence in the love-letter written by Vicky to Sarika was done using the sky-blue coloured ink-pen. The next sentence in the love-letter written by Vicky to Sarika was done using the turquoise blue coloured ink-pen. Manish said he would have married Sarika if he was not already married with his wife and two children. Ayush told Sarika that Manish would have married her if Manish was single. Sarika felt that Manish was actually after her father's money and properties. Sometimes, Sarika was too-demanding and dominant.

Ayush felt that marrying Sarika could be too risky and a bad decision. Ayush imagined what would be the image if Manish would have been on his knees and proposed his so-called love for Sarika. The image is given below for your reference, knowledge and entertainment.

SO ROMANTIC

Manish claimed that he is a very romantic person by heart. Manish said that he had the stamina and an extraordinary capacity to satisfy his wife in the bedroom. Manish said that he had the ability to give long-lasting pleasure to his wife in the bedroom. Manish took his family which includes his wife (with her he was not interested in getting married) and both children to meet Sarika and her parents.

Sarika lived in a huge bungalow. Sarika's father owned many properties and assets. Sarika's father is a very rich person and had no shortage of money. Sarika told Ayush that he had a good chance to settle in life. Sarika mentioned twice in her personal whatsapp chat with Ayush that he had a good chance to settle in life. Ayush assumed that settling in life is about earning a stable income (money) and getting married eventually.

This was just Ayush's assumption and he was not completely sure of what Sarika was actually thinking about him. Sarika had the habit of confusing men by giving them mixed signals of her interest and disinterest in them. Ayush had conviction in the authoritative scriptures like Bhagavata Puran. Ayush had read the following verse, translation and purport from the Bhagavata Puran about marriage.

"किमात्मनानेन जहाति योऽन्ततः
किं रिक्थहारैः स्वजनाख्यदस्युभिः ।
किं जायया संसृतिहेतुभूतया
मर्त्यस्य गेहैः किमिहायुषो व्ययः ॥ ९ ॥

kim ātmanānena jahāti yo 'ntataḥ
kiṁ riktha-hāraiḥ svajanākhya-dasyubhiḥ
kiṁ jāyayā saṁsṛti-hetu-bhūtayā
martyasya gehaiḥ kim ihāyuṣo vyayaḥ

Synonyms

kim — what is the use; ātmanā anena — of this body; jahāti — gives up; yaḥ — which (body); antataḥ — at the end of life; kim — what is the use; riktha-hāraiḥ — the plunderers of wealth; svajana-ākhya-dasyubhiḥ —

they who are actually plunderers but who pass by the name of relatives; kim — what is the use; jāyayā — of a wife; saṁsṛti-hetu-bhūtayā — who is the source of increasing material conditions;

martyasya — of a person sure to die; gehaiḥ — of houses, family and community; kim — what is the use; iha — in which house; āyuṣaḥ — of the duration of life; vyayaḥ — simply wasting.

Translation

What is the use of the material body, which automatically leaves its owner at the end of life? And what is the use of all one's family members, who are actually plunderers taking away money that is useful for the service of the Lord in spiritual opulence? What is the use of a wife? She is only the source of increasing material conditions. And what is the use of family, home, country and community? Attachment for them merely wastes the valuable energy of one's lifetime.

Purport

The Supreme Personality of Godhead, Kṛṣṇa, advises, sarva-dharmān parityajya mām ekaṁ śaraṇaṁ vraja: "Give up all other varieties of religion and just surrender unto Me." The common man does not appreciate such a statement by the Supreme Personality of Godhead because he thinks that during his lifetime his family, society, country, body and relatives are everything.

Why should one give up any one of them and take shelter of the Supreme Personality of Godhead? But from the behavior of great personalities like Prahlāda Mahārāja and Bali Mahārāja we understand that surrendering to the Lord is the right action for an intelligent person. Prahlāda Mahārāja took shelter of Viṣṇu against the will of his father. Similarly, Bali Mahārāja took shelter of Vāmanadeva against the will of his spiritual master, Śukrācārya, and all the leading demons.

People may be surprised that devotees like Prahlāda Mahārāja and Bali Mahārāja could seek shelter of the side of the enemy, giving up the natural affinity for family, hearth and home. In this connection, Bali Mahārāja explains that the body, which is the center of all material activities, is also a foreign element. Even though we want to keep the body fit and helpful to our activities, the body cannot continue eternally.

Although I am the soul, which is eternal, after using the body for some time I have to accept another body (tathā dehāntara-prāptiḥ), according to the laws of nature, unless I render some service with the body for advancement in devotional service. One should not use the body for any other purpose. One must know that if he uses the body for any other purpose he is simply wasting time, for as soon as the time is ripe, the soul will automatically leave the body.

We are very interested in society, friendship and love, but what are they? Those in the garb of friends and relatives merely plunder the hard-earned money of the bewildered soul. Everyone is affectionate toward his wife and is attached to her, but what is this wife? The wife is called strī, which means, "one who expands the material condition." If a person lives without a wife, his material conditions are less extensive. As soon as one marries and is connected with a wife, his material necessities increase.

puṁsaḥ striyā mithunī-bhāvam etaṁ
tayor mitho hṛdaya-granthim āhuḥ
ato gṛha-kṣetra-sutāpta-vittair
janasya moho 'yam ahaṁ mameti

"The attraction between male and female is the basic principle of material existence. On the basis of this misconception, which ties together the hearts of the male and female, one becomes attracted to his body, home, property, children, relatives and wealth. In this way one increases life's illusions and thinks in terms of 'I and mine.'" (Bhāg. 5.5.8) Human life is meant for self-realization, not for increasing unwanted things.

Actually, a wife increases unwanted things. One's lifetime, one's home and everything one has, if not properly used in the service of the Lord, are all sources of material conditions of perpetual suffering under the threefold miseries (adhyātmika, adhibhautika and adhidaivika). Unfortunately, there is no institution in human society for education on this subject.

People are kept in darkness about the goal of life, and thus there is a continuous struggle for existence. We speak of "survival of the fittest," but no one survives, for no one is free under material conditions."[9]

Sarika told Ayush that he would never really know which

9 Prabhupāda, A.C. Bhaktivedānta Swāmi. 'Bhāgavata Purāṇa.' Bhaktivedānta Vedabase, https://vedabase.io/en/library/sb/8/22/9/. Accessed 7 Nov. 2024

girl would like him. Sarika felt that generally girls will not propose a man because of the fear of getting rejected by that man. Anuradha was another employee who worked in that company. Anuradha said that a girl generally has a queen-size huge and fragile female false ego which may get hurt if a man rejects that girl's proposal of love.

Manish insisted and advised Ayush to propose his feelings of love to Sarika on the Valentine's day (14th February). Ayush was born on the 2nd of November. Bollywood actor Shah rukh Khan was also born on the 2nd of November. Sarika had acquired the knowledge of numerology, tarot card reading and was learning astrology. Sarika felt that two is the lucky number and also the ruling number for Ayush.

Sarika was of the opinion that number two represents moon planet. Sarika was ruled by the moon planet because he was born on the 2nd of November. Sarika felt that Ayush had the good qualities of softness, sensitivity, charm and beauty which represents the moon planet in the subject of numerology. Sarika felt that Ayush had the bad qualities of getting offended soon, over-sensitivity and mood swings because moon planet represents the mind of the person.

Sarika felt that Ayush was scared of getting married. Ayush felt that getting married can be very risky in this kaliyug because generally the husband and wife fight a lot after getting married for around one or two years. Ayush felt that this current age of kaliyug is characterized by quarrel, hypocrisy and is an ocean of faults as mentioned in the 12th canto, chapter number three and verse number fifty-one of the scripture named as the Bhagavata puran.

"कलेर्दोषनिधे राजन्नस्ति ह्येको महान् गुणः ।
कीर्तनादेव कृष्णस्य मुक्तसङ्गः परं व्रजेत् ॥ ५१ ॥

kaler doṣa-nidhe rājann
asti hy eko mahān guṇaḥ
kīrtanād eva kṛṣṇasya
mukta-saṅgaḥ paraṁ vrajet

Synonyms

kaleḥ* — *of the Age of Kali; doṣa-nidheḥ* — *in the ocean of faults; rājan* — *O King; asti* — *there is; hi* — *certainly; ekaḥ* — *one; mahān* — *very great; guṇaḥ* — *good quality; kīrtanāt* — *by chanting; eva* — *certainly; kṛṣṇasya* — *of the holy name of Kṛṣṇa; mukta-saṅgaḥ* — *liberated from material bondage; param* — *to the transcendental spiritual kingdom; vrajet* — *one can go.

Translation

My dear King, although Kali-yuga is an ocean of faults, there is still one good quality about this age: Simply by chanting the Hare Kṛṣṇa mahā-mantra, one can become free from material bondage and be promoted to the transcendental kingdom.

Purport

After mentioning the innumerable faults of this Age of Kali, Śukadeva Gosvāmī now mentions its one brilliant aspect. Just as one powerful king can kill innumerable thieves, one brilliant spiritual quality can destroy all the contamination of this age. It is impossible to overestimate the importance of chanting Hare Kṛṣṇa, Hare Kṛṣṇa, Kṛṣṇa Kṛṣṇa, Hare Hare/ Hare Rāma, Hare Rāma, Rāma Rāma, Hare Hare, especially in this fallen age."[10]

10 Prabhupāda, A.C. Bhaktivedānta Swāmi. 'Bhāgavata Purāṇa.' Bhaktivedānta Vedabase, https://vedabase.io/en/library/sb/12/3/51/. Accessed 7 Nov. 2024

Manish felt that there are some ways to be romantic –

1) Material affection – the couple can hold hands and walk together in the jogger's park
2) Head on the shoulders of the man – the girl can keep her head on his shoulders
3) Helping in household affairs – the life-partner may feel special about himself or herself if the spouse helps in the domestic household activities like cooking, cleaning, washing the utensils and clothes.
4) Manish also thought that kissing, hugging and cuddling together are important activities of the married couple.
5) The act of spending quality time with the life-partner is also a way of making her or him feel special.
6) Gifts – giving special gifts on important occasions like marriage anniversary and birthday.
7) Imagination – the spouse can use their imagination to express nice words to care about the life-partner.
8) Hear with attention – communicating effectively with the life-partner is also essential for improving the romance in the married life.
9) Understanding body language – According to the concept of business communication, studying the material body language of the spouse is also very significant.

A pleasant surprise – romance should also include giving a pleasant surprise to your wife or husband by closing their eyes from behind as was showing in a scene of Deepak Tijori from the Bollywood movie named as 'Khiladi'.

Love letter – writing a romantic so-called love-letter to your beloved (***don't ever write with blood)

Candle-light dinner – Manish sir felt that this is an excellent way of reducing the electricity bill and increasing the restaurant bill.

Romantic weekend trips – Manish suggested that a married couple should definitely visit places like Darjeeling and Shimla

An attractive smile – A romantic smile on the face of the couple is equally important.

Pampering – Pampering your spouse with an excellent oil massage can help you in displaying your caring nature.

Romantic conversation – reading romantic shaayari and poetry can also make the life-partner feel extremely special.

A romantic-walk – Manish was of the opinion that a romantic walk especially in the rainy or winter season in the favourite place of the life-partner is also applicable.

(For example – at the marine drive)

Manish felt that taking important decisions of your life only after consulting your romantic partner is also needed.

Ayush was asked by Sarika whether he remembers her mobile number or not. Ayush was honest enough to reply that he was not able to remember Sarika's mobile number because he did not find her interesting at all. Sarika became upset because of such statement was made by Ayush. Ayush knew another employee in that company who was unmarried and desperately looking for a girl to marry.

His name was Raj. Ayush felt that if Sarika agrees to marry Raj, Ayush would be freed from those romantic link-up rumours in that company. Ayush was not interested in developing a romantic relationship with Sarika. Ayush was not interested in marrying Sarika. Sarika said that she was not ready to marry any employee of that company in which she was currently working. Sarika felt that most of the employees of that company were irresponsible regarding performing their official duty.

Manish was disappointed because Sarika was not able to attract Ayush. Ayush was happy because Sarika was leaving that company as she got a new job in some other company. Before resigning from that company, Sarika thrice reminded Ayush that she was planning to join a new company. Sarika wanted to check whether Ayush will initiate a proposal of love to her or not. Ayush did not send any proposal of love to Sarika.

After knowing that Ayush was spiritually very inclined, Sarika tried very hard to impress Ayush by saying that she wanted moksha. One meaning of Moksha was getting permanently out of the repeated cycle of rebirth and death. Ayush was happy that at least Sarika was preparing herself for getting moksha. Ayush had read in the scriptures that in order to get moksha in this current age of kaliyug it is important to chant and hear those holy names of the supreme God which are mentioned in the authentic scriptures.

"कृते यद्ध्यायतो विष्णुं त्रेतायां यजतो मखैः ।
द्वापरे परिचर्यायां कलौ तद्धरिकीर्तनात् ॥ ५२ ॥

kṛte yad dhyāyato viṣṇuṁ
tretāyāṁ yajato makhaiḥ
dvāpare paricaryāyāṁ
kalau tad dhari-kīrtanāt

Synonyms

kṛte — in the Satya-yuga; yat — which; dhyāyataḥ — from meditation; viṣṇum — on Lord Viṣṇu; tretāyām — in the Tretā-yuga; yajataḥ — from worshiping; makhaiḥ — by performing sacrifices; dvāpare — in the age of Dvāpara; paricaryāyām — by worshiping the lotus feet of Kṛṣṇa; kalau — in the Age of Kali; tat — that same result (can be achieved); hari-kīrtanāt — simply by chanting the Hare Kṛṣṇa mahā-mantra.

Translation

Whatever result was obtained in Satya-yuga by meditating on Viṣṇu, in Tretā-yuga by performing sacrifices, and in Dvāpara-yuga by serving the Lord's lotus feet can be obtained in Kali-yuga simply by chanting the Hare Kṛṣṇa mahā-mantra.

Purport

A similar verse is found in the Viṣṇu Purāṇa (6.2.17), and also in the Padma Purāṇa (Uttara-khaṇḍa 72.25) and the Bṛhan-nāradīya Purāṇa (38.97):

dhyāyan kṛte yajan yajñais
tretāyāṁ dvāpare 'rcayan
yad āpnoti tad āpnoti
kalau saṅkīrtya keśavam

"Whatever is achieved by meditation in Satya-yuga, by the performance of sacrifice in Tretā-yuga, and by the worship of Lord Kṛṣṇa's lotus feet in Dvāpara-yuga is obtained in the Age of Kali simply by glorifying the name of Lord Keśava."

Śrīla Jīva Gosvāmī has further quoted from the Brahma-vaivarta Purāṇa concerning the degraded condition of people in Kali-yuga:

ataḥ kalau tapo-yoga-
vidyā-yajñādikāḥ kriyāḥ
sāṅgā bhavanti na kṛtāḥ
kuśalair api dehibhiḥ

"Thus in the Age of Kali the practices of austerity, yoga meditation, Deity worship, sacrifice and so on, along with their various subsidiary functions, are not properly carried out, even by the most expert embodied souls." Śrīla Jīva Gosvāmī has also cited the Cāturmāsya-māhātmya of the Skanda Purāṇa concerning the necessity of chanting Hare Kṛṣṇa in this age:

tathā caivottamaṁ loke
tapaḥ śrī-hari-kīrtanam
kalau yuge viśeṣeṇa
viṣṇu-prītyai samācaret

"In this way the most perfect penance to be executed in this world is the chanting of the name of Lord Śrī Hari. Especially in the Age of Kali, one can satisfy the Supreme Lord Viṣṇu by performing saṅkīrtana." In conclusion, massive propaganda should be made all over the world to induce people to chant the Hare Kṛṣṇa mantra, by which human society can be rescued from the dangerous ocean of the Age of Kali."[11]

11 Prabhupāda, A.C. Bhaktivedānta Swāmi. 'Bhāgavata Purāṇa.' Bhaktivedānta Vedabase, https://vedabase.io/en/library/sb/12/3/52/. Accessed 10 Oct. 2024

IMPORTANT POINTS ABOUT THIS STORY –

1) The Human Birth Is Ideally Meant To Develop Our Permanent Relationship With The Supreme God Which Is Based On The Authoritative Scriptures In All The Religions.

2) Sarika Later Confessed To Ayush That She Was Not So Serious About Obtaining Moksha From The Repeated Cycle Of Rebirth And Death.

3) Ayush Was Intelligent Enough To Understand That Sarika Was Just Trying To Fool Him By Falsely Claiming That She Is A Very Spiritual Person.

4) The Positive Point About Sarika Is That After One And A Half Year, She Said That She Has Started Chanting And Hearing The Hare Krishna Mantra Minimum 108 Times Daily.

5) Ayush Explained To Sarika About The Importance Of Practicing Spiritual Life Because Money Cannot Solve All The Problems In Life.

6) Another Good Point About Sarika Was That She Was An Emotional Person And If She Invested Her Energy In Developing Love For The Supreme God, Her Life Will Become Successful.

7) Manish Was Not Interested In Getting Permanently Out Of The Repeated Cycle Of Rebirth And Death.

8) Manish Had Friendship With Sarika But Such Friendship Should Ideally Be Based On Developing Loving Relationship With The Supreme God For The Eternal Benefit Of People In This Material World.

The actual philosophy of life is mentioned in the scriptures. Whether God really exits or not? What is the logical proof for existence of the supreme God? Whether God stays in the metaphysical or physical world? Scientific proof of rebirth? Why are people suffering in this material world? Such questions are answered in the scriptures which come in the bonafide disciplic succession of spiritual masters and disciples.